The New Jersey Joke Book

The New Jersey Joke Book

Mike Dalton

A CITADEL PRESS BOOK
Published by Carol Publishing Group

A Citadel Press book
Published by Carol Publishing Group
Citadel Press is a registered trademark of Carol Communications,
    Inc.
Editorial, sales and distribution offices, rights and permissions should be
    addressed to Carol Publishing Group,: 120 Enterprise Avenue, Secaucus,
    N.J. 07094
In Canada: Canadian Manda Group, One Atlantic Avenue, Suite 105,
    Toronto, Ontario M6K 3E7

Carol Publishing Group books are available at special discounts for
    bulk purchases, sales promotion, fund-raising, or educational
    purposes. Special editions can be created to specifications. For
    details, contact: Special Sales Department, Carol Publishing
    Group, 120 Enterprise Avenue, Secaucus, N.J. 07094

Manufactured in the United States of America
10 9 8 7 6 5 4 3 2 1

Library of Congress Cataloging-in-Publication Data
Dalton, Mike.
        The New Jersey joke book / Mike Dalton.
            p.   cm.
        "A Citadel Press book."
        ISBN 0-8065-1714-X (pbk.)
        1. American wit and humor--New Jersey.   2. New Jersey--Social life
and customs--Humor.   I. Title.
PN6231.N558D35   1996
818'.5402--dc20   95-19919
                                                                      CIP

Preface

Let me take a moment of your time to say that this book is an absolute outrage! I've lived in New Jersey all my life, and frankly, I'm sick and tired of people making fun of my home state. None of the jokes in this book make any sense to me. New Jerseyans are not dumb rubes who don't know how to drive. And, if New Jersey is so polluted, why is it called the Garden State? Huh? Huh?!

I present these New Jersey jokes merely as an anthropological study—to show the world how an entire people and their fair state have been maligned for hundreds of years. There's nothing funny about New Jersey, or, rather, nothing to make fun of. New Jersey is a wonderful place. Come visit us sometime. Drive on the Turnpike. Shop in our myriad malls. Canoe the Wading River in the Pine Barrens. (Bet you didn't know that more than half of New Jersey is blanketed in unspoiled pine forest?) Sun your buns at the Jersey Shore. And stop making jokes about New Jersey!

You know something, I changed my mind: Do me a favor, put this book back on the shelf. I've had it up to here with people like you who make fun of my state. Don't even bother turning the page!

—Jersey Mike

The New Jersey
Joke Book

There are no New Jersey jokes. New Jersey is a joke.

Facts about New Jersey

STATE BIRD: the green-headed fly.
STATE MOTTO: Under repair. (Also known as the Garbage State.)
STATE VEGETABLE: Karen Ann Quinlan
STATE TREE: the telephone pole.

Who discovered New Jersey?
The Roto-Rooter Man.

What's the capital of New York?
New Jersey

New Jersey: the only state that glows in the dark.

There are two seasons in New Jersey:
Winter and "Under Construction"

The air in New Jersey doesn't blow. It sucks.

You live in Joisey? What exit?

The New Jersey Turnpike is the only road on which you give directions based on the smells you experience along the way. "Turn left at the rotten egg stench, go about two miles, then make a right at the bus exhaust cloud . . ."

What's the difference between garbage and a girl from Weehawken?
Garbage gets picked up . . . sometimes.

Take seventy-five Jersey residents and put them all in one room. What do you have?

A full set of teeth.

What did the Jersey farmer leave his wife in his will?

His entire empire, but she couldn't touch any of it 'til she turned fourteen.

Why are there so many Polacks in Hudson County?

That's where all the bowling alleys are.

A man goes into the Paramus Shop Rite, looking for toilet paper. The clerk stocking the shelves asks him, "What color would you like?" He responds, "Just give me white. I'll color it myself."

If the Olympics were ever held in New Jersey, what would be the ten new events?

Demolition Derby
Name That Noxious Fume contest
Spittin' for Distance
Father/Son I.Q. Challenge
Greased Pig Catching
Front Yard Car and Major Appliance
   Collecting
Shouting Abusive Remarks at Slow
   Drivers in the Fast Lane Marathon

Carjacking
Inbreeding Bang-Off
Billygoat Swimsuit Competition

Real classified ads seen in New Jersey newspapers:

- FOR SALE: Antique desk suitable for lady
  with thick legs and large drawers.
- Vacation Special: Have your home
  exterminated.
- The hotel has bowling alleys, tennis
  courts, comfortable beds, and other
  athletic facilities.

- WANTED: 50 girls for stripping machine operators in factory.
- WANTED: Unmarried girls to pick fresh fruit and produce at night.
- WANTED: Mother's helper, peasant working conditions.
- Our experienced mom will care for your child. Fenced yard, meals, and smacks included.
- Man wanted to work in dynamite factory. Must be willing to travel.
- WANTED: Man to take care of cow that does not smoke or drink.

- Now is your chance to have your ears pierced and get an extra pair to take home, too.
- Have several very old dresses from grandmother in beautiful condition.
- We do not tear your clothing with machinery. We do it carefully by hand.
- Illiterate? Write for free information.
- See ladies blouses. 50% OFF!
- USED CARS: Why go elsewhere to be cheated? Come here first!
- Mixing bowl set designed to please a cook with round bottom for efficient beating.

A real sign posted in the popular take-out restaurant, The Fireplace, in Paramus: DO NOT CARRY TAKE-OUT BOXES BY HANDLES

What do you get when you mate a New Jerseyan with a gorilla?

A retarded gorilla.

How can you tell if someone is from Lodi?
He glows in the dark.

Why don't adolescent girls from New Jersey wear training bras?
Because the wheels irritate their armpits.

Did you hear the latest New Jersey joke?
Careful! I come from New Jersey.
That's okay, I'll tell it slowly.

How do you make a guy from Atlantic City laugh on a Monday?

Tell him a joke on Friday.

Why did the rube from New Jersey follow his ten-year-old to school?

They were in the same class.

What are the three most difficult years of a New Jerseyan's life?

Second grade.

Did you hear about the lady from Montvale who crashed her car into a tree?

She told the cop it wasn't her fault. After all, she did blow the horn.

Definition of "New Jersey Fresh": Tomatoes grown by the soft glow of a hazardous waste dump.

New Jersey produces a unique crossbreed of hick and guido, making it the only state where you can observe guys named Jeb wearing muscle shirts and Dockers, listening to disco in a pickup truck replete with a gun rack.

A promiscuous young couple were frolicking in the backseat of a Chevy Impala. Things were heating up and getting pretty intense. Finally, the girl gasped, "Oh, darling, kiss me where it smells!" So, her beau jumps into the front seat and drives her to New Jersey.

What's the difference between New Jersey and yogurt?
Yogurt has culture.

Why does California have all the lawyers and New Jersey have all the garbage dumps? New Jersey had first choice.

The Statue of Liberty has turned her back on New Jersey.

Think about it: It's free to enter to New Jersey, but you have to pay to leave it!

A guy and a girl are having a drink at a dumpy bar in Asbury Park. (Are there any other kinds of bars in Asbury Park?) She tells him that she's nicknamed all her best body parts after parts of New Jersey. He points to her boobs and says, "What're those?" She answers, "Freehold." "And that?" he asks, pointing to her ass. "That's Point Pleasant," she proclaims. "And I suppose that's Cherry Hill," he says, pointing between her legs. She smiles. "Nope, that's Eatontown."

What is the definition of a New Jersey intellectual?

A farmer who only uses his goats for milk.

What's the difference between New Jersey and hell?

Bruce Springsteen.

What's a New York shopper's favorite position?

Facing Paramus Park Mall.

Did you hear Dr. Kevorkian is offering a special?

Discount plane tickets to New Jersey.

What's the definition of the American dream? Every New Yorker jumping off the World Trade Center with a New Jerseyan under each arm.

I've just returned from Newark. It's the *only* thing to do if you find yourself there.

MAN FROM MAYWOOD: "Honey, how did the car get here in the kitchen?"

LADY FROM MAYWOOD: "It was easy. I just turned left at the dining room."

Many people enjoy being out in the Pine Barrens of New Jersey—a place where there's nothing to do every minute.

The family from Union City had a lovely place in the New Jersey Pine Barrens. It's just twenty minutes from New York City—by phone.

Did you hear about New Jersey's one and only good driver? She always looks both ways before hitting something . . . always slows down when she goes through a red light.

What do you call a pretty lady in Secaucus.
A tourist.

A handsome man in Bayonne? Lost.

The New Jersey State Militia bought one-thousand septic tanks. As soon as they figure out how to drive them, they're going to invade Staten Island.

Why is the suicide rate so low in New Jersey?
It's hard to die when you jump out a basement window.

Did you hear about the New Jersey car pool?
They meet at work.

How did the New Yorker make a fortune in New Jersey?
He sold Cheerios as doughnut seeds.

What are the world's shortest books?
  Successful New Jersey Businesses
  Pollution-Free New Jersey Beaches
  A Tree Grows in Secaucus
  Safe New Jersey Drivers
  A Breath of Fresh New Jersey Air

Why are New Jersey garbage cans painted orange?

So the kids will think they're eating at Howard Johnson's.

What happened to the guy from Bloomfield who used Odor Eaters?

He walked ten paces, then disappeared.

Why did the Hackensack bakery fail?

Every time they tried to put "Happy Birthday" on a cake, they ruined it in the typewriter.

What did God say when he created New Jersey?

"Oh, Shit!"

Did you hear about the *Hindenberg* arrival party?

It got crashed.

(Everybody knows the Hindenberg crashed in Lakewood, New Jersey. Maybe it was the crackerjack ground crew!)

How many Pineys does it take to eat a possum?

Three: One to eat it, two to watch for oncoming cars.

(Pineys are rubes from the Pine Barrens of New Jersey.)

How do you break a New Jerseyan's finger?

Punch him in the nose.

A guy from Cherry Hill locked his keys in the car.

It took the cops three hours to get his family out with the jaws of life.

Another guy from New Jersey (Pennsauken, to be exact) locked his keys in the car. He found a pay phone and called the cops.

"Please hurry," he pleaded. "It looks like it's about to rain and I've got the top down."

COP: Why are you guys pushing your house down the Turnpike?

GUYS: We're trying to jump-start the furnace.

What's the difference between a porcupine and a carful of New Jersey shoppers?

The porcupine has the pricks on the *outside*.

What's thirty miles long and has an I.Q. of 17?
The commute in on the New Jersey Turnpike.

What do you call a New Jerseyan with five-hundred girlfriends?
A cattle farmer.

What's the difference between a girl from Hoboken and a fox?

Oh, I'd say about seven beers.

What's the difference between a girl from Morristown and a lightbulb?

You can screw a lightbulb.

Did you hear about the new New Jersey lottery?
The winner gets a dollar a year for a million years.

Why is there no ice anywhere in New Jersey?
The guy who had the recipe moved to Florida.

New Jersey postcard: Having a great time.
Now where the hell am I?

There was a plane crash in an Edison ceme-
tery.
They recovered 14,000 bodies.

How do you set a guy from Hackensack up
in a small business?
Set him up in a big business . . . and wait.

How did the Giants fan lose $50 on the game?
Easy. He lost $25 on the game and $25 on the replay.

Why is Giants Stadium covered in Astroturf?
So the cheerleaders don't graze.

Did you hear they found Jimmy Hoffa?
He's buried under the thirty-yard-line at Giants Stadium.

How do we know Jesus wasn't born in Newark?

There's no way they would have ever found three wise men and a virgin anywhere near Newark!

What do you call a Pennsylvanian shepherd driving fifty ewes over the Delaware River into New Jersey?

A pimp.

Did you hear about the New Jerseyan who was killed in a pie-eating contest?

The cow stepped on his head.

How many Rutgers football players does it take to screw in a lightbulb?

One, and he even got an A for it.

How many New Jerseyans does it take to screw in a lightbulb?

Answer #1: None. They call the New Yorkers over to do it.

Answer #2: None. They use candles.

Answer #3: Three: One to hold the bulb, one to be a witness, and one to shoot the witness.

(No joke book is complete without a lightbulb joke.)

(. . . or a "chicken crossing the road" joke!)
Why did the chicken cross the Turnpike?
He didn't make it. He was hit by a semi.

Did you hear about the man from West Milford who broke his pelvis raking leaves?
He fell out of the tree.

A man from Morristown came home early from work one day and found his wife with another man. Mr. Morristown was so infuriated, he pulled out a pistol and put the barrel to his own head. His wife and the "other man" began laughing hysterically.

"Quit laughing!" he yelled. "You're next!"

A man from Bricktown was building a garage and went to the lumberyard to buy some two-by-fours. The man at the lumberyard asked him, "How long do you need your two-by-fours?"

"I'm building a garage," Mr. Bricktown said, "so I'll need them for a long time."

NEW JERSEY MOM: I think Billy's spoiled.

NEW JERSEY DAD: Nonsense! All kids from New Jersey smell like that.

A man from Vernon once bought just one winter snow boot. He had heard there was going to be only one foot of snow.

What do you call six New Jerseyans gathered in a circle?

A dope ring.

Did you hear about the man from Toms River who was stabbed twenty times in the head?

He was trying to eat with a fork for the first time.

A plane was nearing Newark Airport when suddenly one of its engines quit. The pilot announced the plane would now be fifteen minutes late. A short time later, a second engine quit. The pilot announced they would be thirty minutes late. After the third engine quit, the pilot announced that they would be an hour late. At that point, the man from Marlboro turned to his wife and said, "Boy, if the forth engine quits, we could be up here all day."

Why don't people from New Jersey eat pickles?

They keep getting their heads caught in the jar.

A Hackensack high school senior won first prize in the Bergen County scholastic test. A reporter from *Record* asked him how he won.

"Easy. The question was, 'How many legs does a hippo have.' I was the closest; I said three."

Did you hear about Joe from Saddle River? He was wandering on the beach at Point Pleasant one morning and found a magic lamp. He released the genie trapped inside, who gave Joe the Midas touch. From that point on, everything Joe touched turned into a muffler.

Two folks from Manalapan were walking along the beach in Ship Bottom when suddenly, a seagull flew over and dropped a "deposit" on one of their heads. The other ran into the beachhouse and ran back with a roll of toilet paper. "Forget it," the bomb victim said. "That bird is probably five miles from here by now."

Next time you're in Parsippany visit the Holiday Inn.
They have a revolving restaurant in the basement.

What has an I.Q. of 7?
Eight New Jerseyans.

A man from Rochelle Park went to the doctor and complained of being listless. The doctor told him to run ten miles a day and call him back in eight days. Eight days later the New Jerseyan called the Doctor and said, "Doc, I sure feel a lot better but I have a problem."

The doctor asked, "You did run like I had told you, didn't you?"

"Yes," said the New Jerseyan. "But now I'm eighty miles from home and I can't find my way back."

A man from Wallington went to another doctor. After extensive examination, the doctor said, "Take these pills two days running, then skip a day. Follow this routine for two weeks, then report back to me."

At the end of the first week, the New Jerseyan went back to the doctor. "I'm tired, Doc," he complained. "All that running and skipping wore me out."

Why doesn't New Jersey have any pharmacists?

They can't find any typewriters that will work on those little round bottles.

Once upon a time, there was a West Milford man who got water skis for his birthday. He had to take them back because he couldn't find a lake with a hill in it.

Did you hear about the New Jersey atheist?
He gave it up because there weren't any holidays.

Did you know . . . ? It takes three New Jerseyans to play hide and go seek.
One hides, and the other two try to figure out who left.

There was a man from Vernon who lived right on the New Jersey border. One day surveyors came to his door and informed him that they had made a mistake years before, and that he now lived in New York State.

"Oh, good," said the Vernonite. "I don't think I can take another one of those New Jersey winters."

Did you hear about the man from Sparta who smiled every time there was lightning?

He thought he was having his picture taken.

What's the difference between a rich Garfield resident and a poor Garfielder?

A rich Garfielder has *two* cars jacked up on his front lawn.

How do you keep a New Jerseyan busy?
Put him in a round room and tell him there's a penny in the corner.

How do you confuse a New Jerseyan?
Throw a bunch of shovels in the corner and tell him to take his pick.

Why do New Jerseyans have such pretty noses?

They're hand-picked.

Why don't they ever give New Jersey workers more than a ten-minute break?

It's too hard to retrain them once the break's over.

Did you hear about the man from Caldwell who stayed up four days and nights studying for his urine test?

FAIR LAWN MAN #1: "You really should pull your shades down. Last night I saw you kissing your wife."

FAIR LAWN MAN #2: "Oh yeah? The joke's on you. I wasn't even home last night!"

Did you hear about the New Jerseyan who wanted to go to the Southside Johnny concert? The tickets cost five dollars in advance and six dollars at the door.

He decided it wasn't worth the eleven-dollar admission.

The Ridgewood man went to Home Depot and bought a chainsaw. Three days later he went back to the store, complaining that the saw wasn't working right. In three days, he was only able to cut down two trees. The clerk pulled the starter cord and the chainsaw started on the first try. Perplexed, the Ridgewoodie said, "What's that sound?"

More real classifieds seen in New Jersey newspapers:

- LOST: Small apricot poodle—Reward. Neutered, like one of the family.
- FOR SALE: Eight puppies from a German Shepherd and an Alaskan Hussy.
- FOR SALE: Great Dames.
- DOG FOR SALE: Eats anything; especially fond of children.
- PIT BULL FOR SALE: Owner deceased.

- FOUR-POSTER BED—Perfect for antique lover.
- A Superb and Inexpensive Restaurant: Fine food expertly served by waitresses in appetizing forms.
- Dinner Special: Chicken or beef $2.25; Turkey $2.35; Children $2.00.

How many Saddle Brook citizens does it take to make popcorn?

Three: One to hold the pan and two to shake the stove.

Did you hear about the New Jerseyan who was so lazy he married a pregnant woman?

The phone rang one day and the man from Glen Rock answered it and quickly hung up. "Who was it?" his wife asked.

He replied, "It was the operator. She said it was long distance from Florida. It told her 'I'll say!' and hung up."

A renowned Glassboro University professor was conducting an experiment regarding the hearing sense of frogs. He cut off one leg and told the frog to jump. It did. He cut off a second leg, then told the frog to jump. It did. The professor then cut off the frog's third leg, and then told it to jump again. The frog did. Then the professor cut the fourth leg off, and this time the frog didn't jump.

The professor concluded that when you cut off all of a frog's legs, it loses its hearing.

MAILMAN TO NEW JERSEYAN: Is this your package? The name is obliterated.

NEW JERSEYAN TO MAILMAN: Can't be. My name's Murray.

Why does every shoe sold in New Jersey have TGIF stamped on it?

It stands for "Toes Go In First."

If you turned a New Jerseyan's shoes over, what would they read?

"This side down."

How does someone from New Jersey put on his underwear?

Yellow in the front, brown in the back.

The man from Readington went on vacation to Hawaii. He got off the plane and the beautiful hostess put a Hawaiian lei around his neck and said, "Aloha from Hawaii."

The New Jerseyan held out his hand, "Murphy from New Jersey. A pleasure to meet you."

A New Jerseyan read in the *Star Ledger* that most accidents occur within ten miles of home. So he moved.

Why do New Jerseyans only smell good on the right side?

Because they haven't found a store that sells "Left Guard."

Why do seagulls fly over New Jersey upside down?

Because they can't find anything worth crapping on.

If you discovered two Santa Clauses on your roof, how could you tell which one was from New Jersey?

He's the one with the Easter Basket.

Definition of a New Jersey hijacker: He hijacks a submarine and demands $500,000 and a parachute.

Next time you see a New Jerseyan with blisters on his face, you'll know what he was doing.

Bobbing for French Fries.

Two Pennsylvanians and a New Jerseyan had a bet on who could stay in a pig sty with pigs the longest. The first Pennsylvanian lasted two days and left. Three days later, the second one left. Two days after that, the pigs left.

In New Jersey, they think Shirley Temple is a synagogue.

Why did the New Jerseyan spend two weeks in the revolving door?

He couldn't find the doorknob.

A reporter asked the Little Falls man what he thought of the Indianapolis 500. "They're all innocent," he replied.

An unemployed Hillsboro man got a job working for the New Jersey Turnpike Authority painting the yellow stripe on the Turnpike. The first day on the job he painted a mile. The second day, half a mile. The third day, a quarter of a mile, and the fourth day, twenty feet. Furious, his boss asked, "How come each day you painted less and less?"

"Each day I got farther and farther away from the bucket."

Ramapo College had Astroturf installed on its football field, and it cost $250,000 more than the Astroturf at Columbia University.

Reason: The New Jerseyans also had a sprinkler system installed.

You'll notice that all New Jersey fire trucks have a Dalmation that rides to the fires with the firemen. That's the only way the New Jerseyans can find the fire hydrants.

One poor Cape May man bought a bottle of aftershave lotion and the very next day was found dead on the bathroom floor. The autopsy revealed that he had slapped himself to death.

The Bricktown man obviously didn't understand when the lady in Houlihan's bar told him she was a lesbian. The New Jerseyan's response was, "Oh, how are things in Beirut?"

A Park Ridge man sat in a carwash one day for three hours because he thought it was raining too hard to drive.

The job application had a blank to be filled in with the date of birth and the year. The Waldwick man filled in: Date: August 16. Year: every year.

There was once a Rutgers football player who heard he was going to be a first-round draft choice. So he fled to Canada.

Two New Jersey state legislators were talking one day. "What do you think we should do about the prostitution bill before the Senate?"

"I think if we owe it, we should pay it."

When New Jersey firemen buy new fire trucks, what do they do with their old fire trucks?

They use them for false alarms.

In Wallington the other day, a New Jerseyan died after refusing artificial respiration.

He said he wanted the real thing.

The New Jerseyan told the librarian he wanted to read a good book. "Do you want something light or heavy?" asked the librarian.

"It doesn't matter. I have my car outside," he answered.

What's dumb, ugly, and rings your doorbell incessantly?

The New Jersey Avon Lady.

A Princeton scientist has found a solution to the water shortage.

He gathered up all the available water and diluted it.

The New Jersey executive knew his job was in jeopardy when they moved him to a smaller office that stopped at each floor. His buddy had it worse: his new office had a toilet, two sinks, and tile on the floor.

New Jerseyans don't eat M&Ms. They get tired of trying to peel them.

One guy from Newton returned his M&Ms, claiming they were defective. They all had W on them.

NEW JERSEY STATE TROOPER NUMBER 1: "He got away, didn't he? Didn't I tell you to cover all exits?"

NEW JERSEY STATE TROOPER NUMBER 2: I did, sir. But I think he must have walked out through one of the entrances."

All along the Las Vegas strip, a man from Chester was running back and forth, putting dimes in parking meters. A curious bystander asked, "What are you doing?"

The New Jerseyan replied, "I love this outdoor gambling."

The Readington man rushed home one night and happily announced to his wife: "Dear, now we don't have to move to a more expensive apartment. The landlord has raised our rent."

A New Jersey pilot was enroute from Newark to Atlantic City with 127 passengers. Bad weather forced them to circle Atlantic City. As the fog continued, they kept circling for almost an hour. Finally, the pilot announced over the P.A. system. "I have some bad news and some good news. The bad news is that we are running out of gas. The good news is, I'm parachuting down to get help."

WILLIAM PATERSON PROFESSOR: "Do you want to help in the fight against malaria?"

NEW JERSEY STUDENT: "Why, what have the Malarians done now?"

An example of a New Jersey matched crystal set: Three empty peanut butter jars with the same label.

There is only one thing wrong with New Jersey coffee.

One month later you're sleepy again.

Did you hear about the intelligent New Jerseyan?

It was just a rumor.

There were two parachutists, one from Connecticut and one from New Jersey. They were making their first jumps. The New Jerseyan jumped first, counted to ten, and pulled the ripcord. His chute opened. The Connecticutter then jumped, counted to ten, pulled the ripcord ... and nothing happened. He then pulled his emergency cord. Again, nothing. Before long, he dropped past Mr. New Jersey. The New Jerseyan looked down at the falling Connecticutter and immediately began unbuckling his chute, hollering, "So, you wanna race, do ya?"

What do 1776 and 1492 have in common?
They're adjoining rooms at the Hasbrouck Heights Hilton.

Wine list in New Jersey restaurant:
   1. Red wine.
   2. White wine.
   (Order by number).

TEACHER: What is an autobiography?

WYCKOFF STUDENT: Erf . . . the life story of a car?

A man from Emerson went into the Midland Bank and told the manager, "I'd like to join your Christmas Club, but I gotta warn you: I won't be able to attend all the meetings."

A man walked into the room to find his New Jersey brother hanging by his ankles. When asked what he was doing, the New Jerseyan reported, "I've had it. I'm trying to commit suicide."

"You dope," said his brother, "you're supposed to put the rope around your neck, not your ankles!"

"I tried that," said Mr. New Jersey, "but I couldn't breathe."

Did you hear about the Westwood man who refused to read the dictionary?

He said he was waiting for it to be made into a movie.

WANTED: 320 acres in Chester to lease between November and March. Want to raise frozen vegetables.

New Jersey Drivers' Etiquette:

Vary your vehicle's speed inversely with the speed limit.

Write the words HELP ME on your back window in red paint. The more it looks like blood, the better.

Laugh a lot. A whole lot.

Stop at the green, go on red.

Honk frequently for no apparent reason.

Never, ever stop for a pedestrian unless he flings himself under your wheels. If he's still causing a commotion, back over him and finish the job.

Whenever possible, stop in the middle of a crosswalk in order to inconvenience as many pedestrians as possible.

Stop and collect roadkill.

Stop and pray to roadkill.

Get in the fast lane then . . . gradually . . . slow . . . down . . . to . . . a . . . stop.

When in doubt, accelerate.

Always look both ways when running a red light.

Never use your directionals. It just confuses other drivers, who are not used to them.

Never pass on the left when you can pass on the right.

How did the blind man find New Jersey?
He followed his nose.

Did you hear about the hooker from the New Jersey Meadowlands?
She gave glow jobs.

What do you call a New Jerseyan who sits in a tree?

Branch manager.

There was once a war between New Yorkers and New Jerseyans.

New Jersey threw dynamite. New York lit it and threw it back.

CONVICT NUMBER 1 IN TRENTON STATE PRISON: What are you in for? I'm in for manslaughter.

CONVICT NUMBER 2: I'm in for barnyard rape. I screwed a pig and it squealed on me.

What does it say on the bottom of all Coke bottles sold in New Jersey?

OPEN OTHER END.

What does it say on the top step of all ladders sold in New Jersey?

STOP!

Why are New Jersey moms so strong?
From raising dumbbells.

How many New Jerseyans does it take to take a bath?

Thirty-seven: One to sit in the tub and thirty-six to spit on him.

What does a New Jersey mom say to her unwed pregnant daughter?

Look on the bright side. Maybe it's not yours.

Why are New Jersey jokes so short?
So Kentuckians can understand them, too.

The girl from New Jersey was so dumb that when her boyfriend blew in her ear, she said "Thanks for the refill."

What's the difference between McDonald's and a hooker from Hackensack?

McDonald's has only served fifty billion people.

A used car dealer in Elmwood Park got arrested last week. He was caught turning back all the fuel gauges on his cars.

What's smarter than two New Jerseyans?
One New Jerseyan.

Why is a New Jersey dictionary so cheap?
It's not in alphabetical order.

That man started out as an underweight, inex-
perienced, unselfconfident, ugly dishwasher
from Secaucus. Unfortunately, he never lived
up to his early promise.

A farm in New Jersey was ten miles long by three miles wide.

The farmer grew spaghetti.

The New Jersey Shore is so dull.

One day the tide went out, and it never came back.

You know how polluted New Jersey water is?

Last year, a reservoir dam gave way, but the water didn't.

You can walk past the water and hear it coughing.

If God was going to give the world an enema, he'd start in New Jersey.

The student from Wallington was so excited about graduating grammar school, he could hardly shave.

The man from Hawthorne came home soaking wet from the car wash.
He forgot to take the car.

Assorted bumper stickers seen on New Jersey cars:

MY CHILD CAN BEAT UP YOUR HONOR STUDENT

CATS FLATTENED WHILE YOU WATCH

STUPID PEOPLE SHOULDN'T BREED

IF YOU DON'T LIKE MY DRIVING, GET OFF THE
SIDEWALK

MY KARMA JUST RAN OVER YOUR DOGMA

USE CAUTION WHEN PASSING—DRIVER
CHEWING TOBACCO

IF YOU CAN READ THIS BUMPER STICKER,
YOU'RE IN RANGE

THIS VEHICLE SWERVES AND HITS PEDESTRIANS
AT RANDOM

What did the man from Roselle do when the doctor told him he had sugar in his urine?
Pissed on his corn flakes.

What if the state of New Jersey doesn't pay its garbage bill?
They stop delivery.

They had a Miss New Jersey beauty pageant, and the winner came in third.

What's a fuck-off?
A tie breaker at the Miss New Jersey pageant.

The dying wish of an old man from Whiting was to be buried at sea.
Tragically, his two sons drowned digging his grave.

Definition of a New Jersey shishkabob?
A flame arrow through a garbage can.

A man from Ridgewood went down to Atlantic City to shoot craps.
Too bad his wife didn't know how to cook them.

A man from Rutherford was ice fishing. He cut his hole and dropped in his line. Suddenly, he heard a booming voice, "There's no fish in there!"

Fearing it was the voice of God, Mr. Rutherford moved to another section of the ice, sawed a new hole, and heard the voice again. "There's no fish in there!"

He moved to another spot, began cutting another hole, and suddenly lights came on. And the announcer came over the PA again: "You're in the Meadowlands Arena. There are no fish in the Devils' home rink!"

How do you sink the New Jersey Navy?
Put the boats in the water.

Who wears a dirty white robe and rides a pig
through the streets?
Lawrence of Paterson.

What is a New Jersey matched luggage set?
Three shopping bags from Pathmark.

How come nobody makes Kool Aid in Rochelle Park?

They can't figure out how to get a quart of water in those little envelopes.

What does New York State do with its old garbage trucks?

Sell them to New Jersey as campers.

What does a Closter businessman carry in his briefcase?

His briefs, of course.

Why do Jersey girls always flunk their driver's tests?

Every time the car stalls, they jump into the backseat and take off their clothes.

The man from New Jersey cleaned his ears, and his head caved in.

The student from Rutgers was majoring in animal husbandry, until they caught him at it.

What's the definition of gross ignorance?
One hundred and forty-four people from New Jersey.

There's a factory in Clifton that manufactures burglar alarms.
Yesterday it was robbed.

We don't worry about crime in the streets in New Jersey. It makes house calls.

NEW JERSEY GUY NUMBER 1: My wife drives like lightning.

NEW JERSEY GUY NUMBER 2: You mean she drives fast?

NEW JERSEY GUY NUMBER 1: No, she hits trees.

My wife came up with a new kind of drive-way. It's called a lawn.

She must hate the phone company. She keeps knocking down their poles.

The New Jersey State art museum was sup-posed to open last week, but the frame broke.

Let me tell you above the dumbest guy in the world. Surprise! He just happened to live in New Jersey.

You'd give him a penny for his thoughts, and you'd have change coming.

He had a hemorrhoid operation, and at the end of it, they found a brain tumor.

He was once given the key to the city by the mayor of Fair Lawn and he locked himself out.

He changed his mind once. The new one didn't work any better.

He tried to get a job as an idiot, but he was overqualified.

New Jersey's only Olympic athlete wasn't much smarter.

His specialty was javelin catching.

What do you call removing a wart from a New Jerseyan's butt?

Brain surgery.

The New Jersey State aquarium in Camden features fish indigenous to the state. Be sure to visit the next time you want to see polly-wogs wallowing around in radioactive pond scum.

Why are rectal thermometers banned in New Jersey?
They cause brain damage.

In New Jersey, they stop garbage deliveries if you fall behind in your payments.

How can you tell when it's a New Jersey funeral?
The garbage trucks all drive with their lights on.

How can you tell if you're at a New Jersey used car lot?

All the cars' fuel gauges have been turned back.

Why do New Jerseyans have doormats in their houses?

So they can clean off their shoes before going outside and dirtying up the rest of the world.

How can you tell when it's snowing at Newark Airport?

They put chains around all the propellers.

What do you call a cow in New Jersey?

Somebody's date.

What's a contaminated landfill?

A New Jersey health spa.

What's the difference between a New Jersey woman and a bear?

About fifty pounds and a fur coat.

How do you sink a New Jersey submarine?

Knock on the hatch.

Did you hear about the New Jersey jigsaw puzzle?
It had one piece. Some people were still confused.

What's a New Jersey vacation?
Two days and six nights.

How did two New Jersey guys get their luggage mixed up at Newark Airport?
They both had K-Mart shopping bags.

The garbage on our block hasn't been picked up in so long, it was declared a landmark.

The New York (really New Jersey!) Giants have a lot on the ball.
Unfortunately, it's never their hands.

I wouldn't call Hackensack a safe town. One guy held up a bank and was mugged on the way to the getaway car.

The Piney drank a jug of moonshine every day. He died at ninety-six. When he was cremated, it took a week to put out the fire.

A New Jersey woman ran after a garbage truck, "Am I too late for the garbage?" To which the garbageman replied, "No, jump right in."

What's the best way to get rid of garbage?
Gift wrap it and leave it in the parking lot at Paramus Park.

Piney walked into a hotel lobby. The doorman said, "You'll have to wipe your shoes." To which the Piney retorted: "I ain't goin' home to fetch them just for that."

The beaches at the Jersey Shore really get crowded in the summer. Last Fourth of July in Belmar, they didn't have one drowning. Just five crushings.

New Jersey is so dull that passing trains have stopped blowing their horns, because it wakes everybody up.

New Jersey is so dull that drugstores there sell postcards showing scenes from other states.

New Jersey is so dull that a night on the town in New Jersey lasts about fourteen minutes.

The only way to have fun in New Jersey is to move away.

Did you hear the one about the gal from New Milford who took up nude painting?
She got pneumonia and died.

How to parallel park, New Jersey style:

Step 1: Back up until you hit the car behind you.

Step 2: Pull forward until you hit the car in front of you.

Even insects in New Jersey are dumb. A mosquito once bit an Atlantic City showgirl in the arm.

There are so many muggers in Union City you can walk twenty blocks without leaving the scene of a crime.

The only way to improve upon New Jersey is to tear it down and put up a slum.

I went to an outdoor cafe in Hoboken.
I was mugged by the busboy.

The first thing that strikes an out-of-towner in Jersey City is the accent. The second is a New Jersey driver.

The word is that English will soon be the most popular language in the world. Now if somebody would only tell Dumont.

MR. NEW JERSEY: What happened to the car?

MRS. NEW JERSEY: I hit a cow.

MR. NEW JERSEY: There was a cow in the middle of the road?

MRS. NEW JERSEY: No, I had to chase it out of the barn.

The fledgling New Jersey driver failed her driving test because of one slight mistake. She ran over the man giving the test.

A New Jersey woman driver went through three red lights in a row. They were on the truck in front of her.

A moron from New Jersey once put his hand in a lion's mouth to see if the lion had any teeth. The lion closed his mouth to see if the man had any fingers.

A UFO landed at Newark Airport. The aliens were safe, but they lost their luggage.

Folks can gamble just about anywhere in Atlantic City. One poor slob went into a laundromat and lost his laundry.

A woman from Maywood, told her husband, "Be an angel and let me drive." He did, and he is.

The air in New Jersey is so polluted that when you lay out, instead of getting a nice tan, you get a beautiful stain.

The babe from New Jersey was so dumb, she put beer in her waterbed so she could have a foam mattress.

A scene from English class at Bergen Community College, (a.k.a. Bergen Comedy) in Paramus.

PROFESSOR: Did you write this poem all by yourself?

NEW JERSEY STUDENT: Every word of it.

PROFESSOR: I'm glad to meet you, Mr. Poe. I thought you were long dead.

My family and I went to the beach in Seaside yesterday. We walked up and down the beach for hours, collecting drift garbage.

Talk about tough neighborhoods . . .

Where I live in Paterson, nobody asks you the time. They just take your watch.

My high school had recess twice a day so we could carry out the wounded.

It's so smoggy, you can get mugged for your cough drops.

There's a good reason why so many people from New Jersey have a stupid look on their face: They're stupid.

A tornado touched down in New Jersey the other day and did $12 million dollars' worth of improvements.

A man discovered he had six months to live. The doctor suggested he sell his house in Wyoming and move to New Jersey.

"Will that help me to live longer?" he asked.

"No," the doctor replied, "but it will *seem* longer."

And now a word from New Jersey: HELP!!

More Humor Books From Carol Publishing Group

dvanced Backstabbing and Mudslinging chniques by George Hayduke, paperback .95 (#40560)

rst, Kill All the Lawyers, compiled by Bill dler, paper $8.95 (#51587)

etting Even by George Hayduke, ersized paper $12.95 (#40314)

etting Even 2 by George Hayduke, ersized paper $12.95 (#40337)

New York City Was the World, by John rschbaum, paper $8.95 (#51573)

ake 'em Pay by George Hayduke, per $8.95 (#40421)

ake My Day by George Hayduke, per $7.95 (#40464)

ayhem by George Hayduke, paper $7.95 40565)

en Just Don't Understand: A Woman's Dat-g Dictionary by Nancy Linn-Desmond, paper 3.95 (#51666)

ore of the World's Best Dirty Jokes by Mr. "J", aper $5.95 (#50710)

999 Lies For Every Occasion by Jo Donnelly, paper $8.95 (#51672)

"O'Brien and Fitzgerald Walk Into A Bar...": The World's Best Irish Jokes by Mr. "O's", paper $7.95 (#51663)

Revenge by George Hayduke, oversized paper $14.95 (#40353)

Revenge Tactics From the Master of Mayhem by George Hayduke, paper $8.95 (#40575)

Still More of the World's Best Dirty Jokes by Mr. "J", paper $3.95 (#50834)

365 Funniest Golf Jokes compiled by Fred Gefen, paper $7.95 (#51688)

"Three Rabbis In A Rowboat...": The World's Best Jewish Humor by A. Stanley Kramer, paper $9.95 (#51775)

201 Ways to Get Even With Your Boss by Linda Higgins, paper $8.95 (#51570)

Underground Office Humor by S.E. Mills, paper $9.95 (#51567)

The World's Dirtiest Dirty Jokes by Mr. "J", paper $7.95 (#51478)

ces subject to change; books subject to availability